Psalms for the Church Year
Volume Two

Marty Haugen

Music Collection

G.I.A. Publications, Inc.   7404 So. Mason Ave., Chicago, Illinois 60638

Introduction

The collection *Psalms for the Church Year* by David Haas and myself was published by GIA five years ago as an attempt to provide a resource of the common psalm settings usable by both traditional choral/keyboard ensembles as well as smaller scholas relying largely on guitar and/or piano. For this second volume, I have tried to fill the largest gaps in the Sunday lectionary left by volume one. In addition, I have tried to set the psalms most closely connected to the various rites of the church (The Rite of Christian Initiation of Adults, Baptism, Confirmation, Penance, Marriage, Anointing of the Sick, Funerals). There is an index on the following pages of how settings from the two volumes can be used for the Sundays of the year, major feasts and the Rites. Whenever it seemed desirable, an alternate refrain has been provided.

In this volume, instrumental introductions have been included for several psalms. These are always optional, and each psalm can easily begin with the intonation of the refrain by a cantor, which is repeated by all. It was my intention that the introductions would be most often used when the setting is presented at times other than as the psalm response (eg. as a communion or processional song).

Thanks to GIA for their continuing support and assistance in helping me present this music in the most pastoral way possible. It is my hope that these settings might be useful for your own prayer and the prayer of your community.

A collection of woodwind parts is available separately from the publisher, G-3261 INST.

Soli Deo Gloria
Marty Haugen
March 25, 1988

NOTICE

The unauthorized copying or rearranging of the words or music of this edition, for any reason whatsoever, is a direct violation of the copyright law for which the person responsible, as well as the institution he or she represents, is subject to prosecution. This includes hand copying, photo copying, even the making of just one copy. To do so is to deprive the persons whose names appear on this edition, as well as the publisher and its employees, of just income.

For permission to make copies, write to the publisher.

The English translation of the psalm responses for Psalms 33, 40, 89, and 96 from *Lectionary for Mass* © 1969, International Committee on English in the Liturgy, Inc. All rights reserved.

© Copyright 1988 by G.I.A. Publications, Inc.
7404 So. Mason Ave., Chicago, IL 60638
International Copyright Secured   All Rights Reserved   Printed in U.S.A.

TABLE OF CONTENTS – VOLUME II

Psalm 16	You Will Show Me the Path of Life	6
Psalm 23	Shepherd Me, O God	9
Psalm 33	Let Your Mercy Be on Us	14
	The Earth Is Full of the Goodness of God	17
Psalm 40	Here Am I, O God	18
Psalm 42, 43	Like a Deer That Longs	22
Psalm 80, 85, Luke 1	Lord, Make Us Turn to You	25
Psalm 89	For Ever I Will Sing	27
Psalm 96	Today Is Born Our Savior	32
Psalm 126	God Has Done Great Things for Us	38
Psalm 128	Blest Are Those Who Love You	43
Psalm 136	Your Love Is Never Ending	46
Psalm 146, 147	Bless the Lord, My Soul	48
	Lord, Come and Save Us	51
Exodus 15	I Will Sing to My God	52
Isaiah 12	With Joy You Shall Draw Water	54
Luke 1	My Soul Proclaims Your Greatness	57
Reprint boxes for congregational use		60

Index of Psalm Settings in the Sunday Lectionary

This is an index of all the Sundays of the church year, plus the major feasts and rites of the church. A psalm marked (*) indicates that a suggested common psalm has been substituted here for the psalm from the lectionary for that Sunday or feast.

The psalms are indicated by psalm number, by volume and by page number. For example, "Ps. 122-1 (83)" is Psalm 122 from volume one of *Psalms for the Church Year*, page 83.

PSALMS FOR THE SUNDAYS AND FEASTS OF THE YEAR

Advent
1-A) Ps. 122-I (83)	1-B) Ps. 80-II (25)	1-C) Ps. 25-I (4)
2-A) Ps. 72-I (16)	2-B) Ps. 85-I (8)	2-C) Ps. 126-II (38)
3-A) Ps. 146-II (48)	3-B) Lk. 1-II (57)	3-C) Is. 12-II (54)
4-A) Ps. 85-I (8)*	4-B) Ps. 89-II (27)	4-C) Ps. 80-II (25)

Christmastide (A,B,C)
Vigil mass	Ps. 89-II (27)
Mass at midnight	Ps. 96-II (32)
Mass at dawn	Ps. 98-I (12)*
Mass during the day	Ps. 98-I (12)
Holy Family	Ps. 128-II (43)
Octave of Christmas	Ps. 98-I (12)*
Christmas-2	Ps. 147-II (51)
Epiphany	Ps. 72-I (16)
Baptism of the Lord	Ps. 27-I (59)

Lent
1-A) Ps. 51-I (20)	1-B) Ps. 25-I (4)	1-C) Ps. 91-I (24)
2-A) Ps. 33-II (14)	2-B) Ps. 130-I (27)*	2-C) Ps. 27-I (59)
3-A) Ps. 95-I (70)	3-B) Ps. 19-I (57)	3-C) Ps. 103-I (76)
4-A) Ps. 23-II (14)	4-B) Ps. 130-I (27)*	4-C) Ps. 34-I (62)
5-A) Ps. 130-I (27)	5-B) Ps. 51-I (20)	5-C) Ps. 126-II (38)

Holy Week (A,B,C)
Passion Sunday	Ps. 22-I (30)
Chrism Mass	Ps. 89-II (27)
Holy Thursday	Ps. 116-I (33)
Good Friday	Ps. 31-I (36)

Easter Vigil (A,B,C)
Ps. 104-I (53)	Ps. 33-II (17)	Ps. 16-II (6)
Ex. 15-II (52)	Is. 12-II (54)	Ps. 19-I (57)
Ps. 42, 42-II (22)	Ps. 51-I (20)	Ps. 118-I (45)
		Ps. 136-II (46)

Easter
1-A) Ps. 118-I (45)	1-B) Ps. 118-I (45)	1-C) Ps. 118-I (45)
2-A) Ps. 118-I (45)	2-B) Ps. 118-I (45)	2-C) Ps. 118-I (45)
3-A) Ps. 16-II (6)	2-B) Ps. 118-I (45)*	3-C) Ps. 66-I (42)*
4-A) Ps. 23-II (9)	4-B) Ps. 118-I (45)	4-C) Ps. 100-I (74)
5-A) Ps. 33-II (14)	5-B) Ps. 22-I (30)	5-C) Ps. 145-I (80)
6-A) Ps. 66-I (42)	6-B) Ps. 98-I (12)	6-C) Ps. 66-1 (42)*
7-A) Ps. 27-I (59)	7-B) Ps. 103-I (76)	7-C) Ps. 47-I (51)*

Ascension
A) Ps. 47-I (51)	B) Ps. 47-I (51)	C) Ps. 47-I (51)

Pentecost (A,B,C)
Vigil Mass/Sunday	Ps. 104-I (53)

Trinity
A) Ps. 103-I (76)*	B) Ps. 33-II (14)	C) Ps. 27-I (59)*

Corpus Christi
A) Ps. 147-II (48)	B) Ps. 116-I (33)	C) Ps. 116-I (33)*

Ordinary Time

2-A) Ps. 40-II (18)	2-B) Ps. 40-II (18)	2-C) Ps. 96-II (32)
3-A) Ps. 27-I (59)	3-B) Ps. 25-I (4)	3-C) Ps. 19-I (57)
4-A) Ps. 146-II (48)	4-B) Ps. 95-I (70)	4-C) Ps. 27-I (59)*
5-A) Ps. 34-I (62)*	5-B) Ps. 147-II (51)	5-C) Ps. 27-I (59)*
6-A) Ps. 19-I (57)*	6-B) Ps. 103-I (76)*	6-C) Ps. 63-I (67)*
7-A) Ps. 103-I (76)	7-B) Ps. 103-I (76)*	7-C) Ps. 103-I)76)
8-A) Ps. 63-I (67)*	8-B) Ps. 103-I (76)	8-C) Ps. 19-I (57)*
9-A) Ps. 19-I (57)*	9-B) Ps. 19-I (57)*	9-C) Ps. 100-I (74)*
10-A) Ps. 95-I (70)*	10-B) Ps. 130-I (27)	10-C) Ps. 103-I (76)*
11-A) Ps. 100-I (74)	11-B) Ps. 34-I (62)*	11-C) Ps. 103-I (76)*
12-A) Ps. 27-I (59)*	12-B) Ps. 145-I (80)*	12-C) Ps. 63-I (67)
13-A) Ps. 89-II (27)	13-B) Ps. 34-I (62)*	13-C) Ps. 16-II (6)
14-A) Ps. 145-I (80)	14-B) Ps. 85-I (70)*	14-C) Ps. 66-I (42)
15-A) Ps. 19-I (57)*	15-B) Ps. 85-I (8)	15-C) Ps. 63-I (67)*
16-A) Ps. 103-I (76)*	16-B) Ps. 23-II (9)	16-C) Ps. 27-I (59)*
17-A) Ps. 19-I (57)*	17-B) Ps. 145-I (80)	17-C) Ps. 103-I (76)*
18-A) Ps. 145-I (80)	18-B) Ps. 34-I (62)*	18-C) Ps. 95-I (70)
19-A) Ps. 85-I (8)	19-B) Ps. 34-I (62)	19-C) Ps. 33-II (14)
20-A) Ps. 100-I (74)*	20-B) Ps. 34-I (62)	20-C) Ps. 40-II (18)
21-A) Ps. 63-I (67)*	21-B) Ps. 34-I (62)	21-C) Ps. 145-I (80)*
22-A) Ps. 63-I (67)	22-B) Ps. 19-I (57)*	22-C) Ps. 63-I (67)*
23-A) Ps. 95-I (70)	23-B) Ps. 146-II (48)	23-C) Ps. 63-I (67)*
24-A) Ps. 103-I (74)	24-B) Ps. 27-I (59)*	24-C) Ps. 51-I (20)
25-A) Ps. 145-I (80)	25-B) Ps. 27-I (59)*	25-C) Ps. 34-I (62)*
26-A) Ps. 25-I (4)	26-B) Ps. 19-I (57)	26-C) Ps. 146-II (48)
27-A) Ps. 80-II (25)	27-B) Ps. 128-II (43)	27-C) Ps. 95-I (70)
28-A) Ps. 23-II (9)	28-B) Ps. 63-I (67)*	28-C) Ps. 98-I (12)
29-A) Ps. 96-II (32)	29-B) Ps. 33-II (14)	29-C) Ps. 27-I (59)*
30-A) Ps. 103-I (76)*	30-B) Ps. 126-II (38)	30-C) Ps. 34-I (62)
31-A) Ps. 103-I (76)*	31-B) Ps. 19-I (57)*	31-C) Ps. 145-I (80)
32-A) Ps. 63-I (67)	32-B) Ps. 146-II (48)	32-C) Ps. 145-I (80)
33-A) Ps. 128-II (43)	33-B) Ps. 16-II (6)	33-C) Ps. 98-I (12)

Christ the King

    A) Ps. 23-II (9)   B) Ps. 98-I (12)*   C) Ps. 122-I (83)

PSALMS FOR VARIOUS RITES

The Rite of Christian Initiation of Adults (RCIA)

  Admission to catechumenate   Ps. 33-II (14)
  Scrutinies   1st) Ps. 95-I (70)   2nd) Ps. 23-II (9)   3rd) Ps. 130-I (27)

Infant Baptism

    Ps. 23-II (9)   Ps. 27-I (59)   Ps. 34-I (62)

Adult Baptism

    Ps. 27-I (59)   Ps. 63-I (67)

Confirmation

    Ps. 23-II (9)   Ps. 96-II (32)   Ps. 104-I (53)   Ps. 145-I (80)

Penance

    Ps. 25-I (4)   Ps. 51-I (20)   Ps. 95-I (70)   Ps. 130-I (27)

Marriage

    Ps. 33-II (17)   Ps. 34-I (62)   Ps. 103-I (76)   Ps. 128-II (43)

Anointing of the Sick

    Ps. 25-I (4)   Ps. 27-I (59)   Ps. 42, 43-II (22)   Ps. 63-I (67)
    Ps. 103-I (76)

Funerals

    Ps. 23-II (9)   Ps. 25-I (4)   Ps. 27-I (59)   Ps. 42, 43-II (22)
    Ps. 63-I (67)   Ps. 103-I (76)

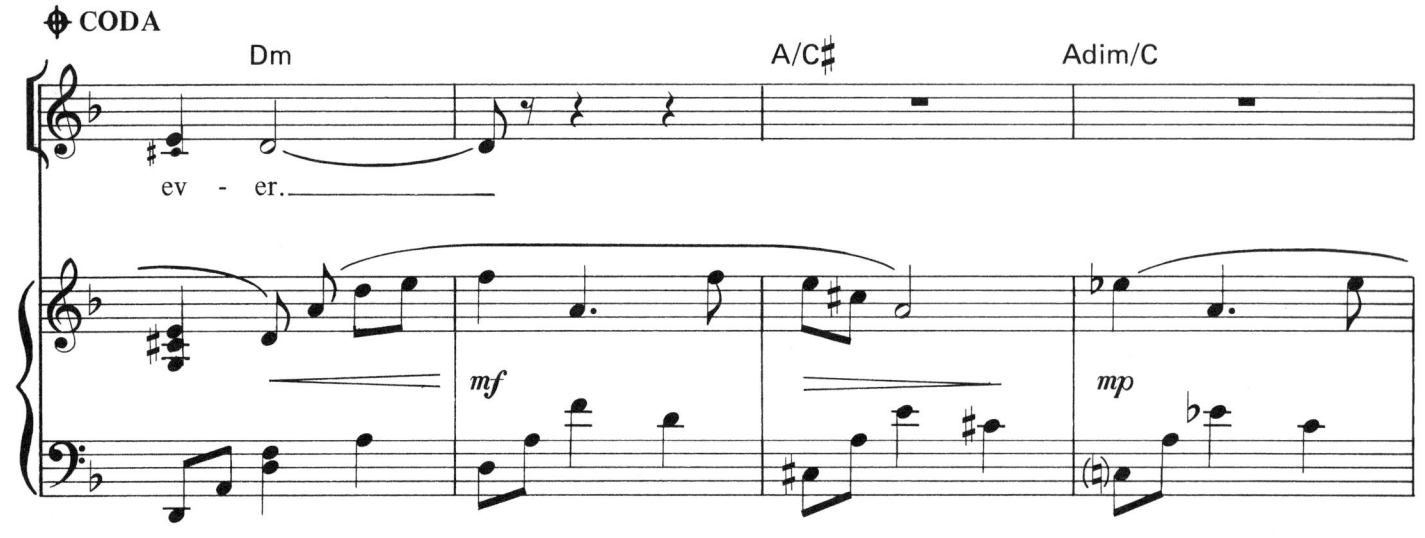
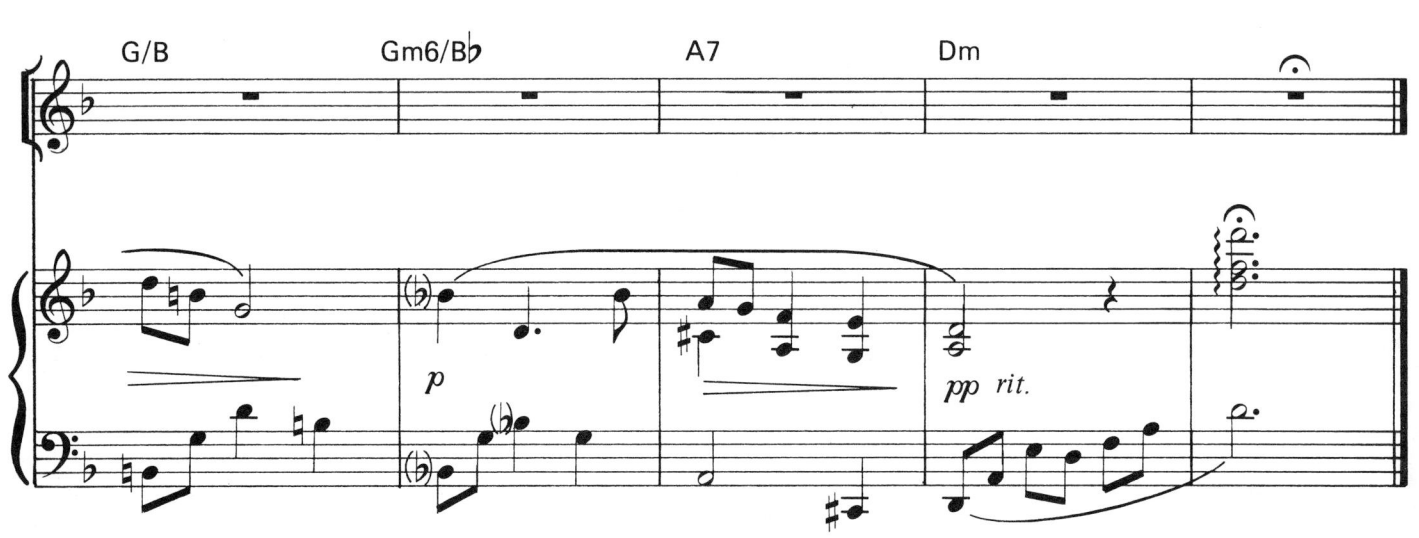

CHORDS FOR "YOU WILL SHOW ME THE PATH OF LIFE"

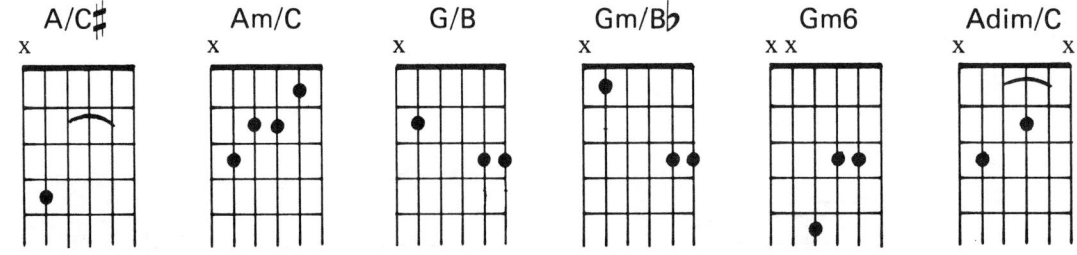

SHEPHERD ME, O GOD

Psalm 23

Marty Haugen

© 1987 by G.I.A. Publications, Inc., Chicago. All Rights Reserved.

1.2.3.5
4.
(Am7) (Bm7)
B♭m7 Cm7
(Em)
Fm
(Am/E)
B♭m/F
(Em7)
Fm7
(A/E)
B♭/F
(Em)
Fm
D/F♯
E♭/G
(G)
A♭
death in-to life.
life.
To verses 1, 2, 3, 5
To verse 4
death to life.
life.
To verse 4
To verses 1, 2, 3, 5

VERSES 1, 2, 3:

(Em)
Fm
(Am/E)
B♭m/F
(Em7)
Fm7
(A/E)
B♭/F
(Em)
Fm
(Am/E)
B♭m/F
mp
1. God is my shep-herd, so noth-ing shall I want, I rest in the mead-ows of
2. Gen-tly you raise me and heal my wea-ry soul, you lead me by path-ways of
3. Though I should wan-der the val - ley of death, I fear no e - vil, for

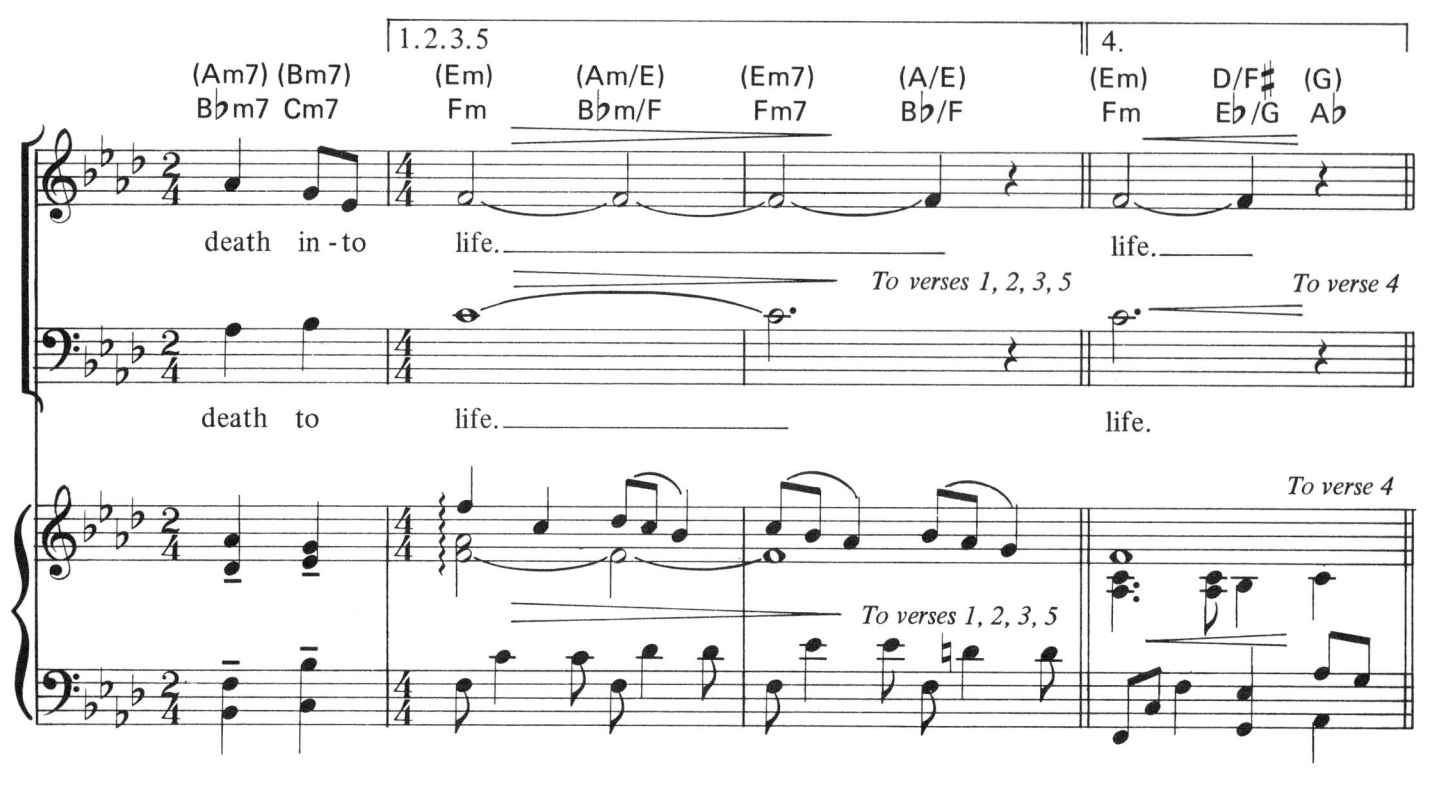

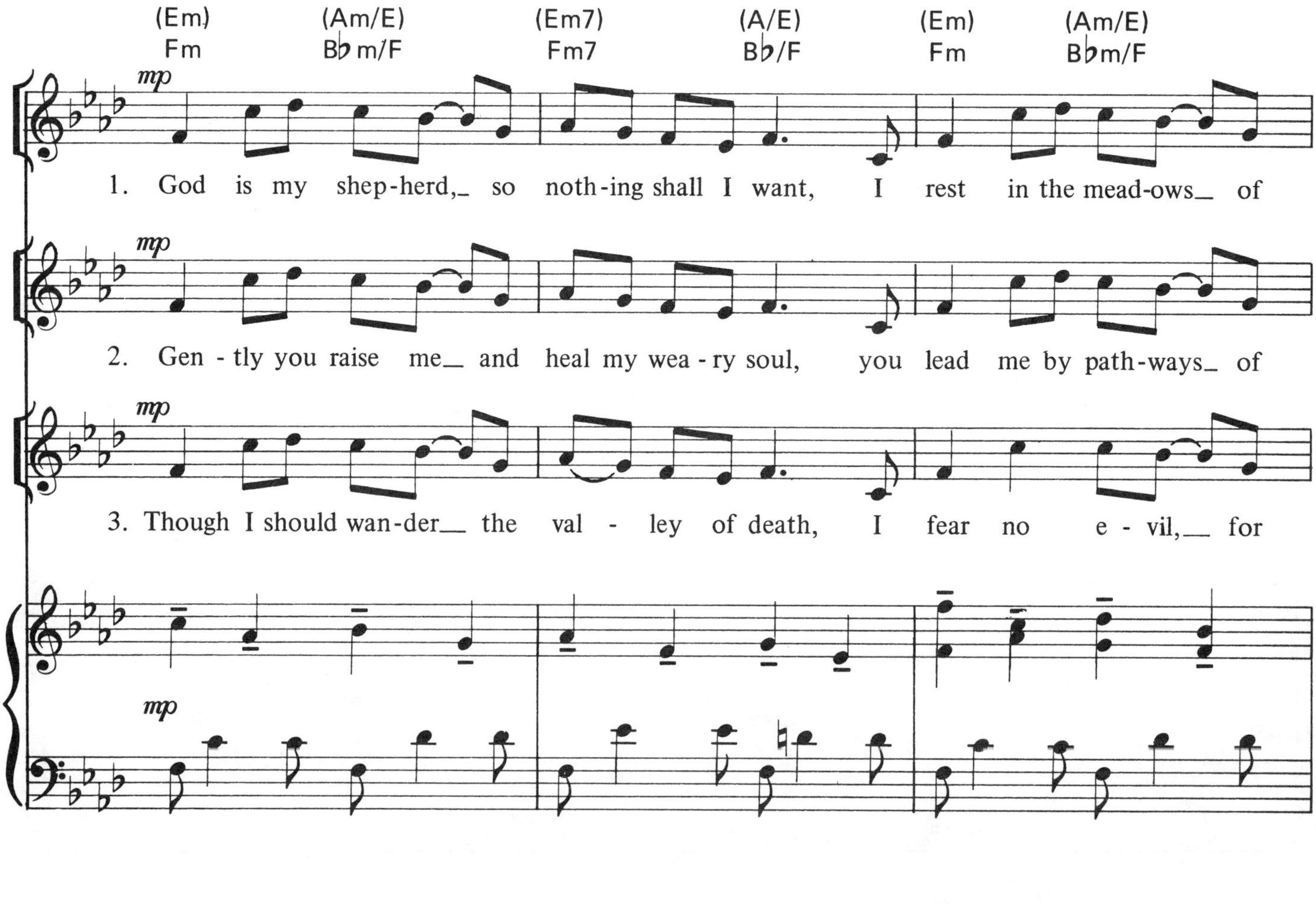

LET YOUR MERCY BE ON US

Psalm 33
Marty Haugen

INTRODUCTION/REFRAIN/CODA:

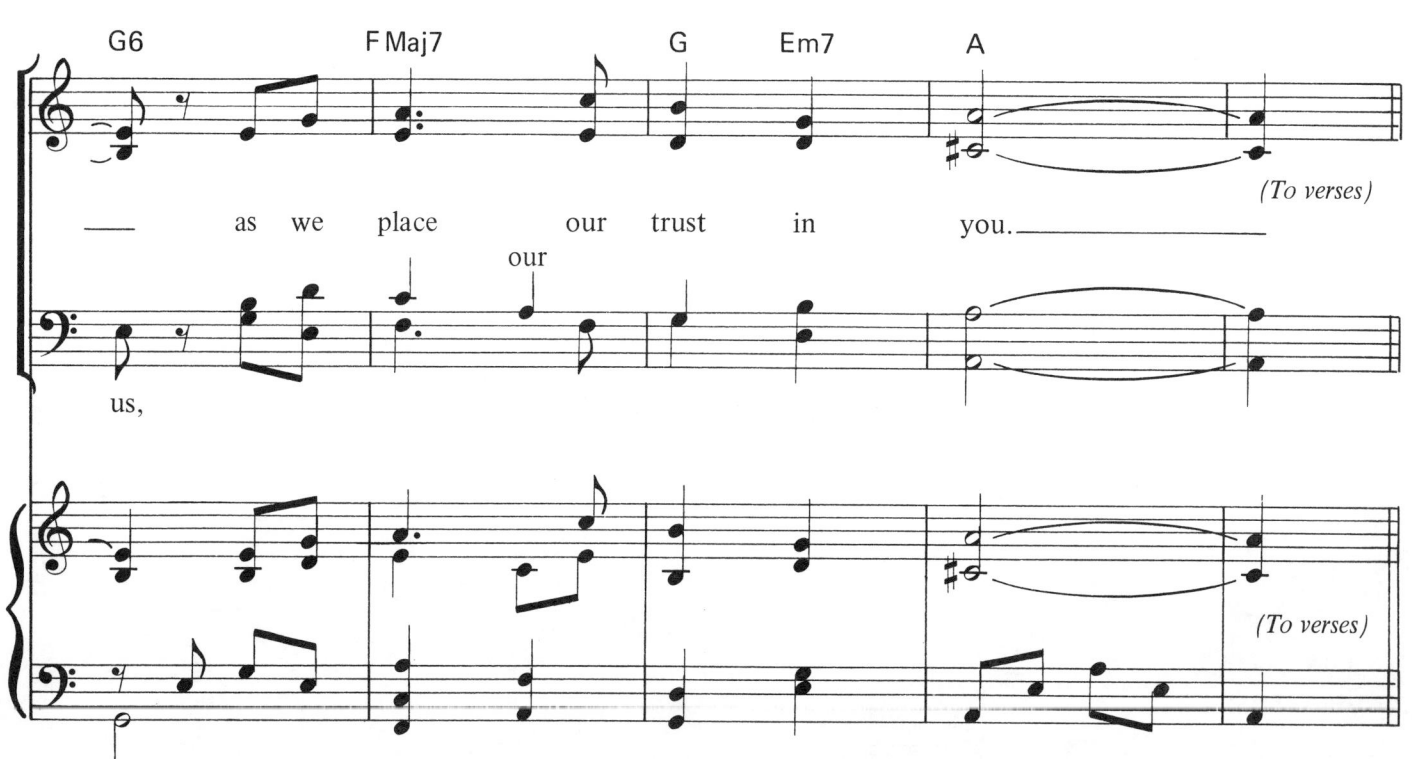

Psalm response from the *Lectionary for Mass* © 1969, International Committee on English in the Liturgy, Inc. All rights reserved.
© 1988 by G.I.A. Publications, Inc. All Rights Reserved.

THE EARTH IS FULL OF THE GOODNESS OF GOD
(Alternate Refrain)

Psalm 33

Marty Haugen

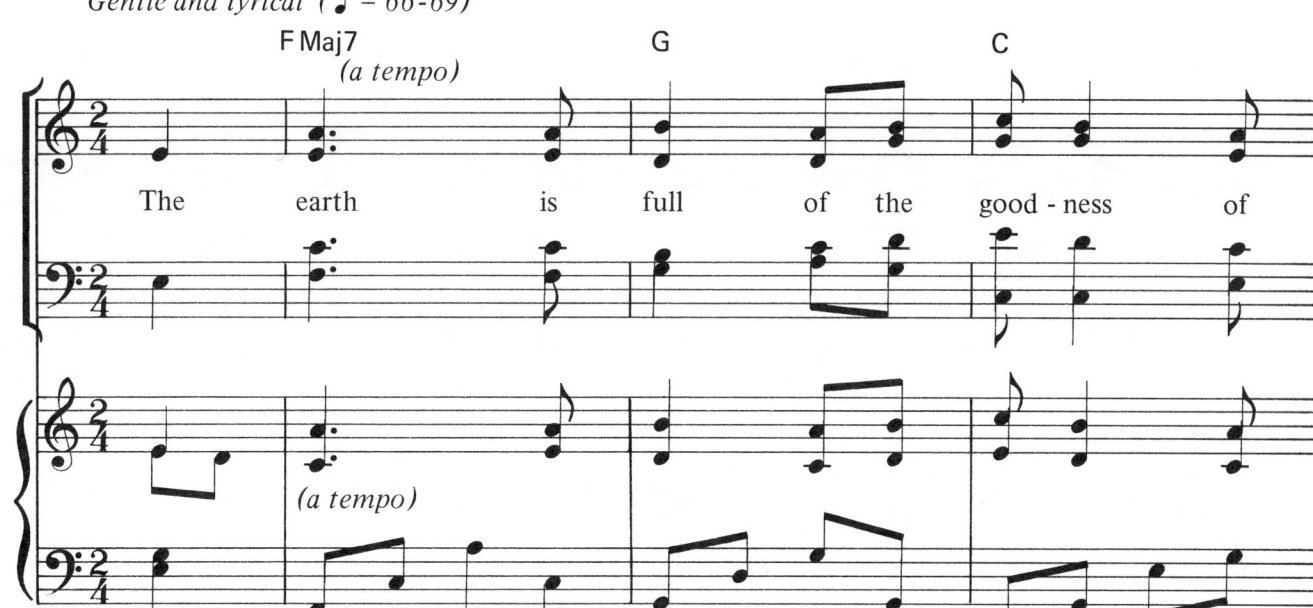

**CHORDS FOR "LET YOUR MERCY BE ON US"/
"THE EARTH IS FULL OF THE GOODNESS OF GOD"**

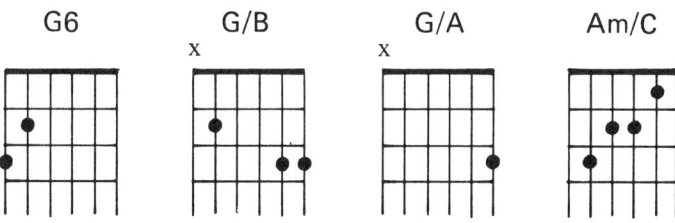

Psalm response from the *Lectionary for Mass* © 1969, International Committee on English in the Liturgy, Inc. All rights reserved.
© 1988 by G.I.A. Publications, Inc. All Rights Reserved.

HERE AM I, O GOD

Psalm 40
Marty Haugen

CHORDS FOR "HERE AM I, O GOD"

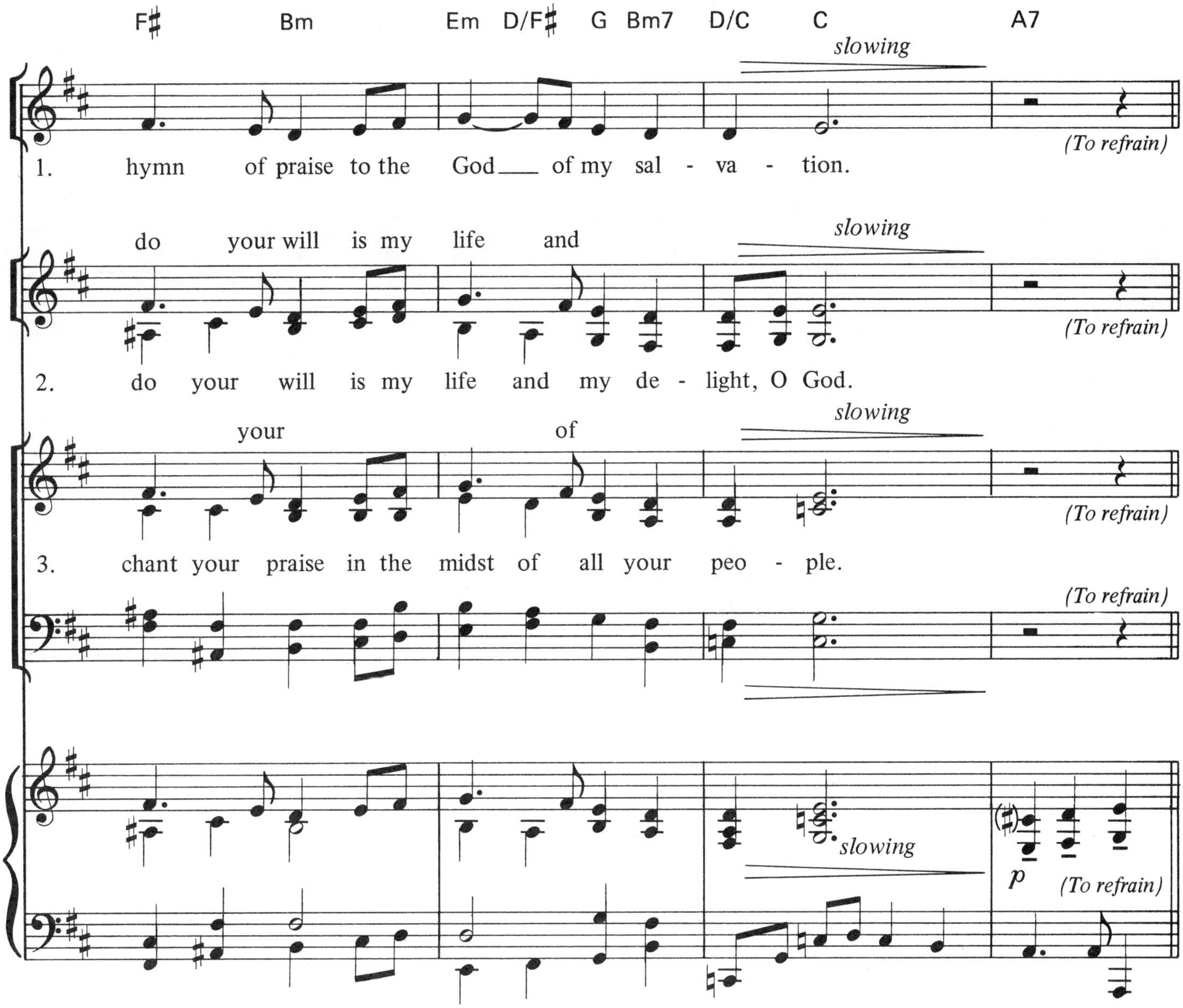

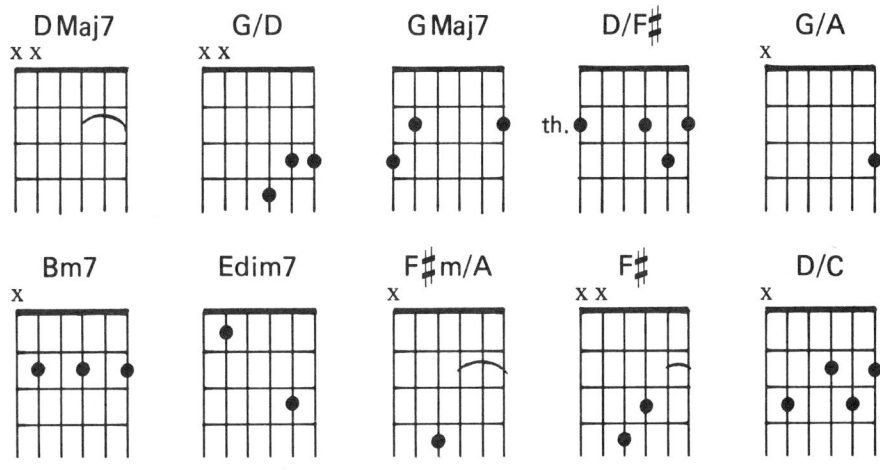

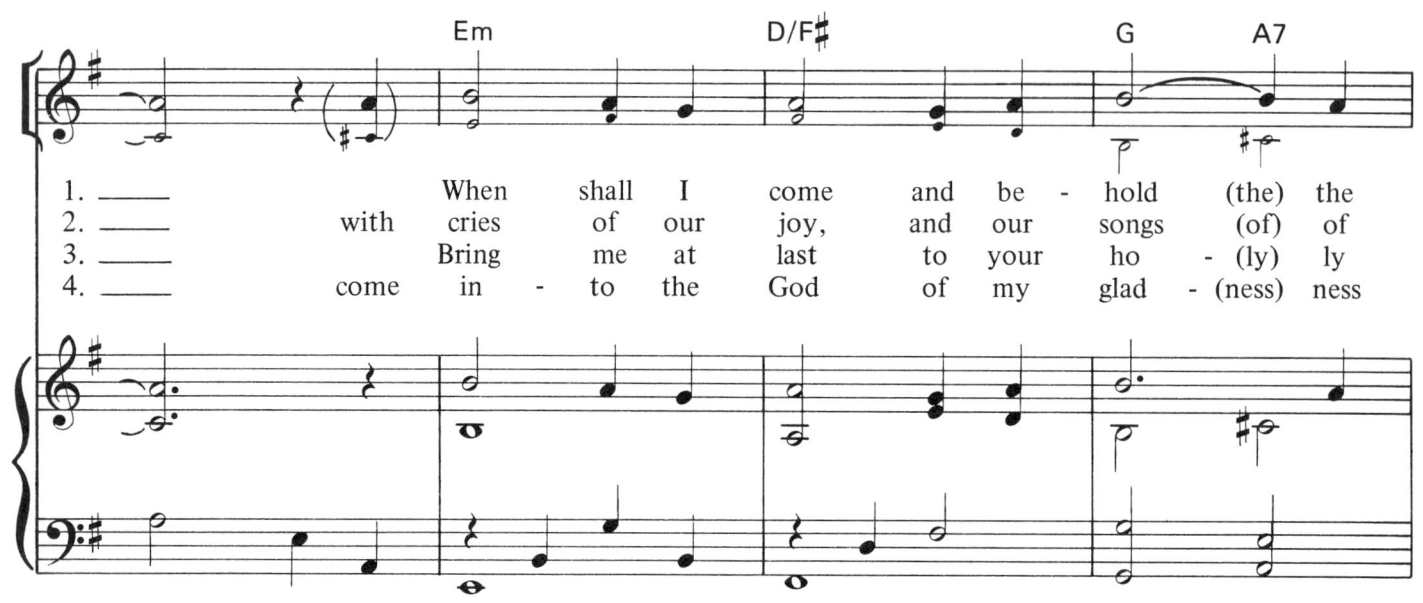

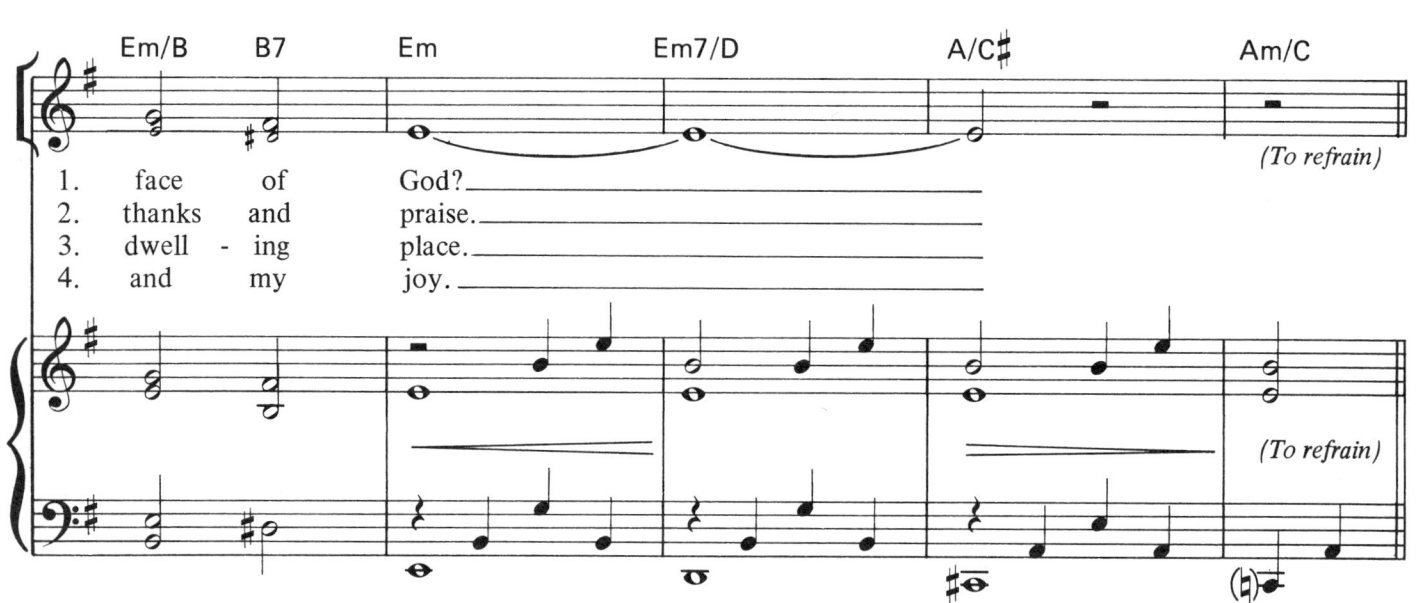

CHORDS FOR "LIKE A DEER THAT LONGS"

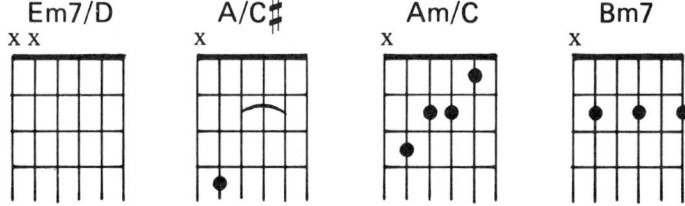

LORD, MAKE US TURN TO YOU

Psalms 80, 85; Luke 1

Marty Haugen

© 1982 by G.I.A. Publications, Inc. All Rights Reserved.

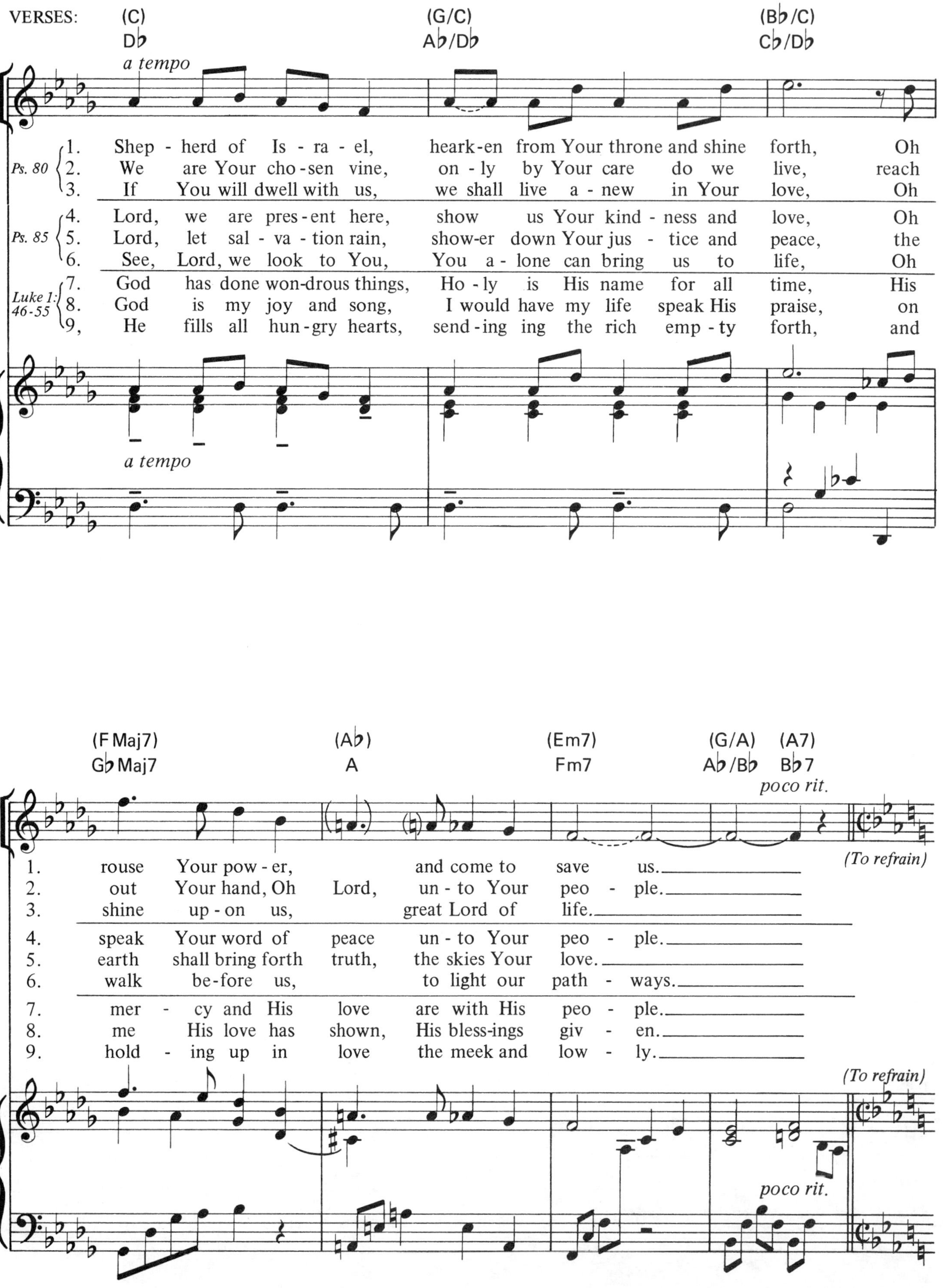
VERSES:
(C) D♭ (G/C) A♭/D♭ (B♭/C) C♭/D♭
a tempo
Ps. 80
1. Shep - herd of Is - ra - el, heark-en from Your throne and shine forth, Oh
2. We are Your cho-sen vine, on - ly by Your care do we live, reach
3. If You will dwell with us, we shall live a - new in Your love, Oh
Ps. 85
4. Lord, we are pres-ent here, show us Your kind - ness and love, Oh
5. Lord, let sal - va - tion rain, show-er down Your jus - tice and peace, the
6. See, Lord, we look to You, You a - lone can bring us to life, Oh
Luke 1: 46-55
7. God has done won-drous things, Ho - ly is His name for all time, His
8. God is my joy and song, I would have my life speak His praise, on
9, He fills all hun-gry hearts, send-ing ing the rich emp - ty forth, and
a tempo
(F Maj7) G♭Maj7 (A♭) A (Em7) Fm7 (G/A) A♭/B♭ (A7) B♭7
poco rit.
1. rouse Your pow - er, and come to save us.
2. out Your hand, Oh Lord, un - to Your peo - ple.
3. shine up - on us, great Lord of life.
4. speak Your word of peace un - to Your peo - ple.
5. earth shall bring forth truth, the skies Your love.
6. walk be-fore us, to light our path - ways.
7. mer - cy and His love are with His peo - ple.
8. me His love has shown, His bless-ings giv - en.
9. hold - ing up in love the meek and low - ly.
(To refrain)
(To refrain)
poco rit.

30

VERSE 2:

* A solo cantor should sing the treble part.

TODAY IS BORN OUR SAVIOR

Psalm 96

Marty Haugen

*N.B. Play E♭ first time only, other times E♮.

Psalm response from the *Lectionary for Mass* © 1969, International Committee on English in the Liturgy, Inc. All rights reserved.
© 1988 by G.I.A. Publications, Inc. All Rights Reserved.

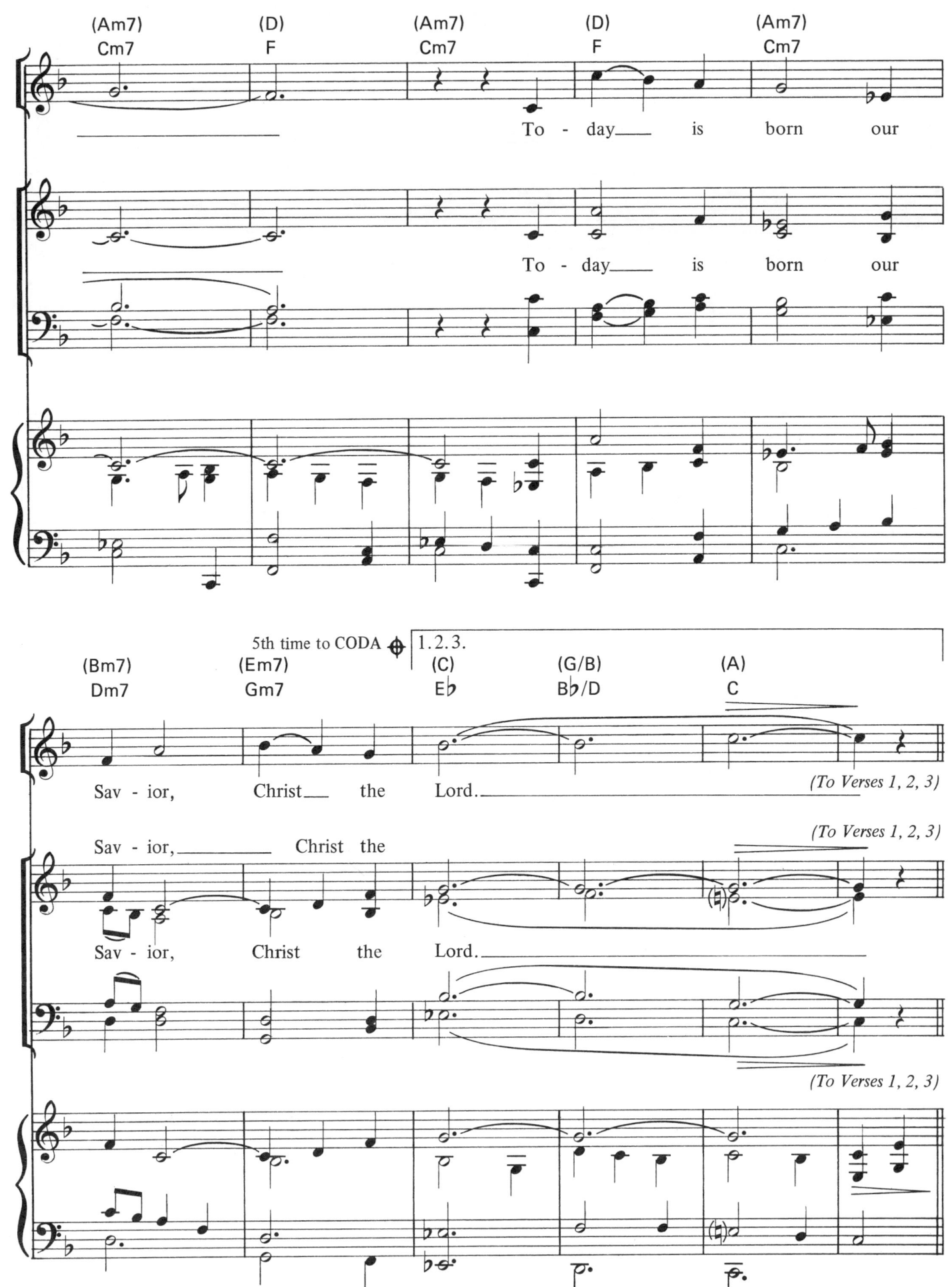

4. (C) / Eb

(G/B) / Bb/D

(To Verse 4)

Lord.

(To Verse 4)

Lord.

(To Verse 4)

(To Verse 4)

VERSES 1, 2, 3:

(Bm7) / Dm7   (D7) / F7   (G) / Bb   (D/F#) / F/A   (Bb) / Db

1. Sing out to God a new song,_____ Sing out to
2. An-nounce God's sal-va-tion for-ev-er,_____ and glo-ry pro-
3. Let us re-joice in our Sav-ior,_____ who has come now to

GOD HAS DONE GREAT THINGS FOR US

Psalm 126
Marty Haugen

© 1988 by G.I.A. Publications, Inc. All Rights Reserved.

REFRAIN:

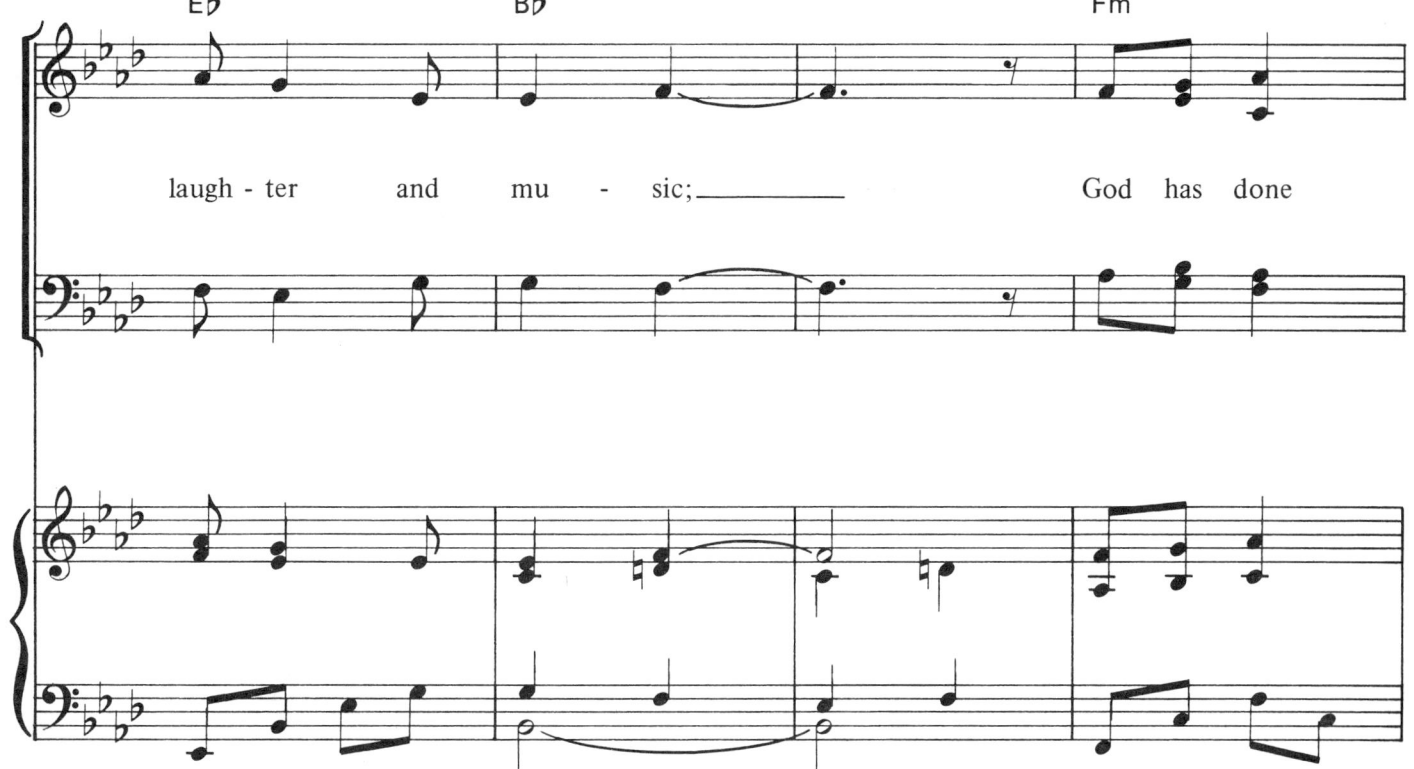

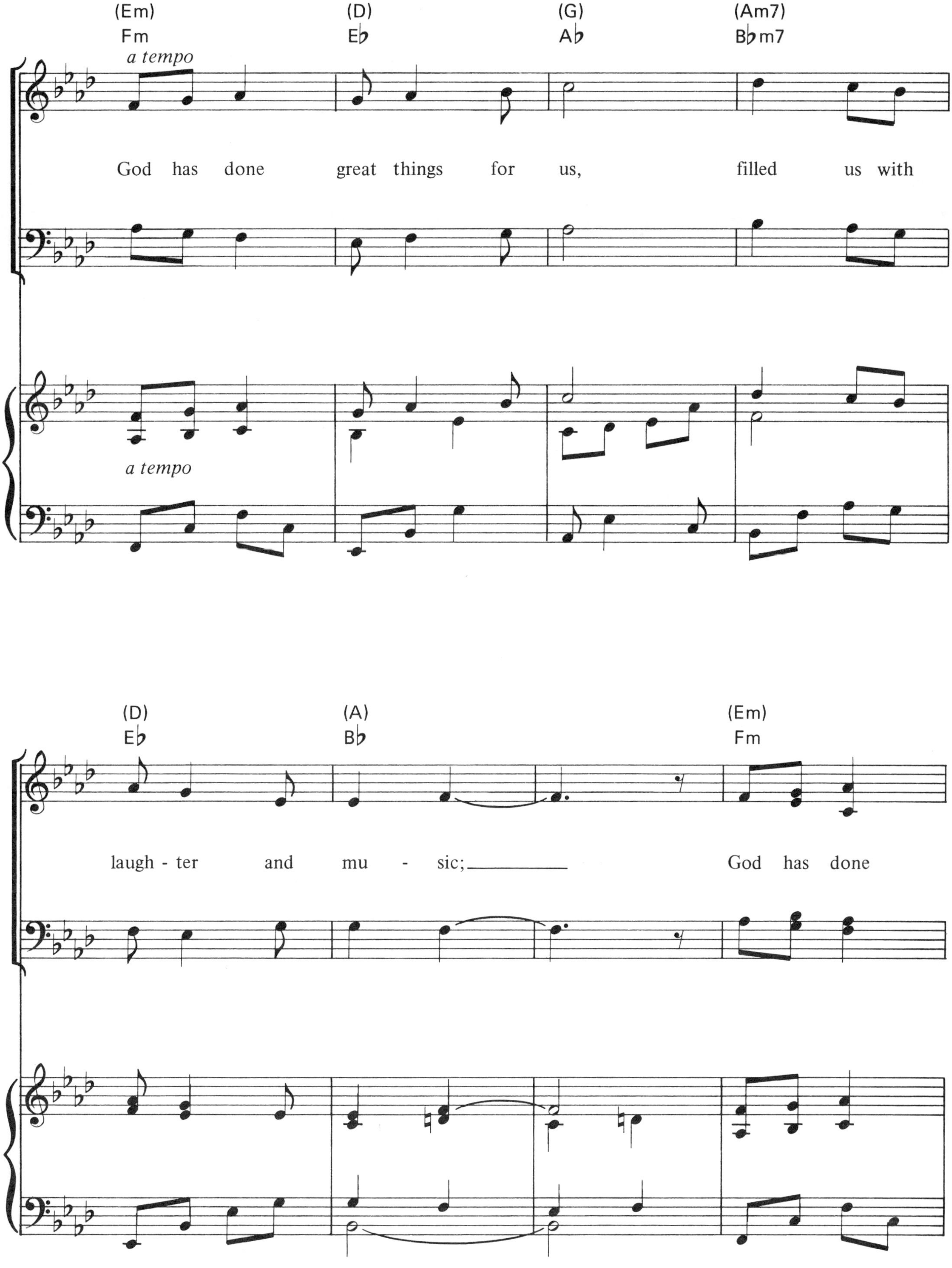
(Em) (D) (G) (Am7)
Fm E♭ A♭ B♭m7
a tempo
God has done great things for us, filled us with
a tempo
(D) (A) (Em)
E♭ B♭ Fm
laugh - ter and mu - sic; God has done

For Cameron Patrick Hall

BLEST ARE THOSE WHO LOVE YOU

Psalm 128

Marty Haugen

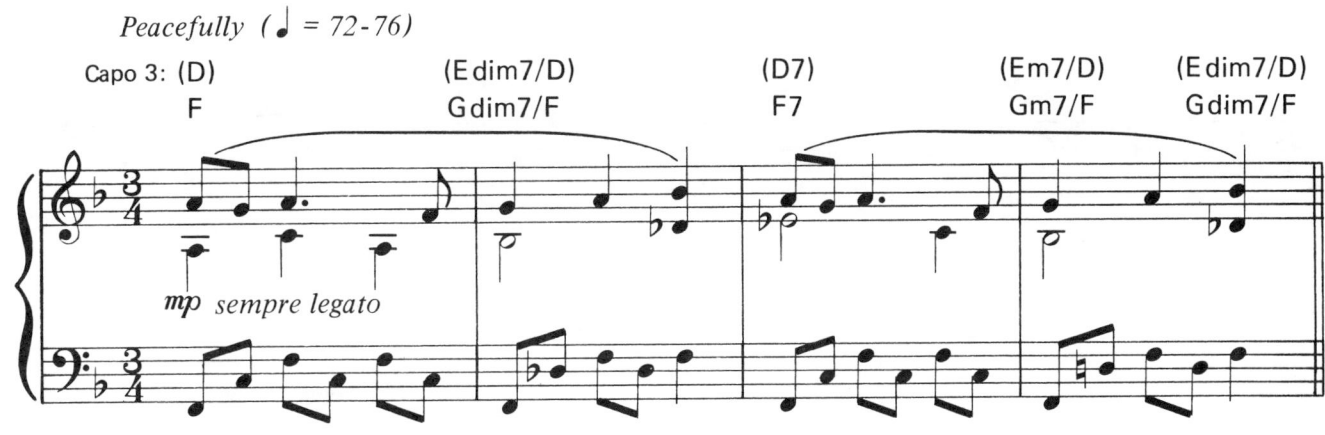

© 1988 by G.I.A. Publications, Inc. All Rights Reserved.

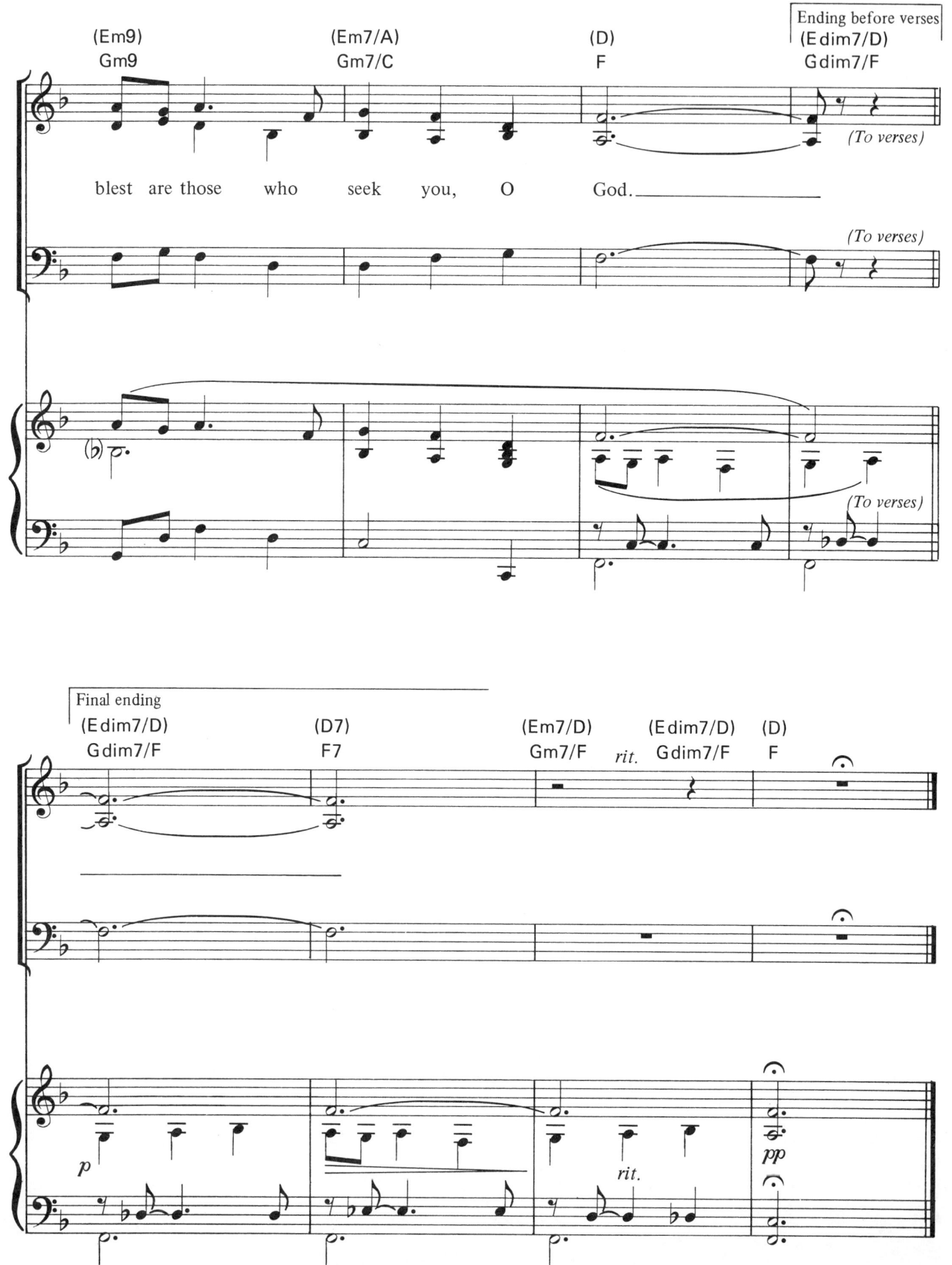

YOUR LOVE IS NEVER ENDING

Words and Music by
Marty Haugen

Psalm 136

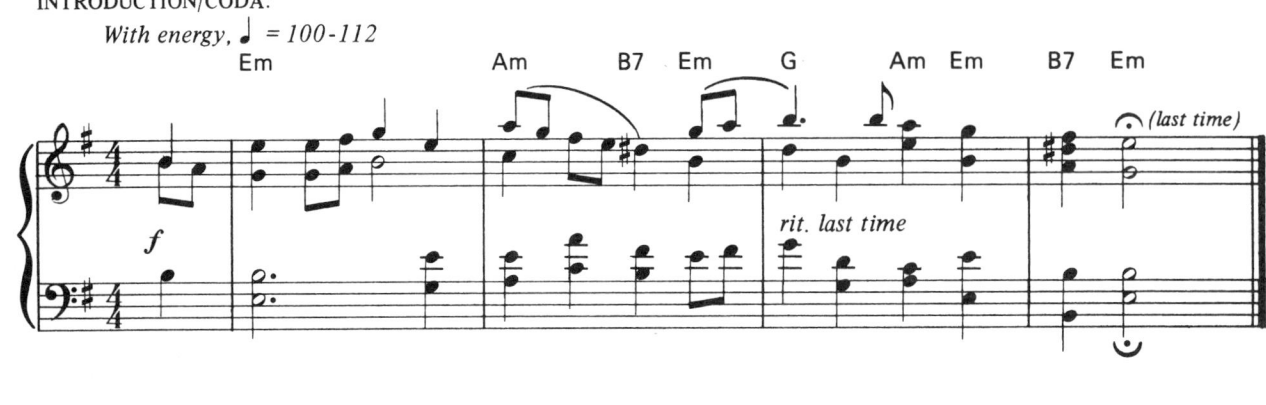

1. We give thanks un-to you, O God___ of___ might:
2. In your wis-dom and love you shaped___ the___ skies:
3. You have filled all the skies with glo___-ry and light:
4. From of old you have led your peo___-ple in faith:
5. You de-liv-ered the ones who called___ un-to you:
6. You have o-pened the sea and brought your peo-ple through:
7. You re-mem-ber your pro-mise age___ to___ age:
8. You give food and life to all___ liv-ing things:

for your love is nev-er end-ing,

(Hum or Ooh)_____ for your love is nev-er end-ing,

© 1987 by G.I.A. Publications, Inc. All Rights Reserved.

LORD, COME AND SAVE US
(Alternate Refrain)

Psalm 146   Marty Haugen

REFRAIN:

Lord, come and save us, Lord, come and save us, Lord, come and save us.

CHORDS FOR "BLESS THE LORD, MY SOUL/LORD, COME AND SAVE US"

© 1988 by G.I.A. Publications, Inc. All Rights Reserved.

I WILL SING TO MY GOD

Exodus 15
Marty Haugen

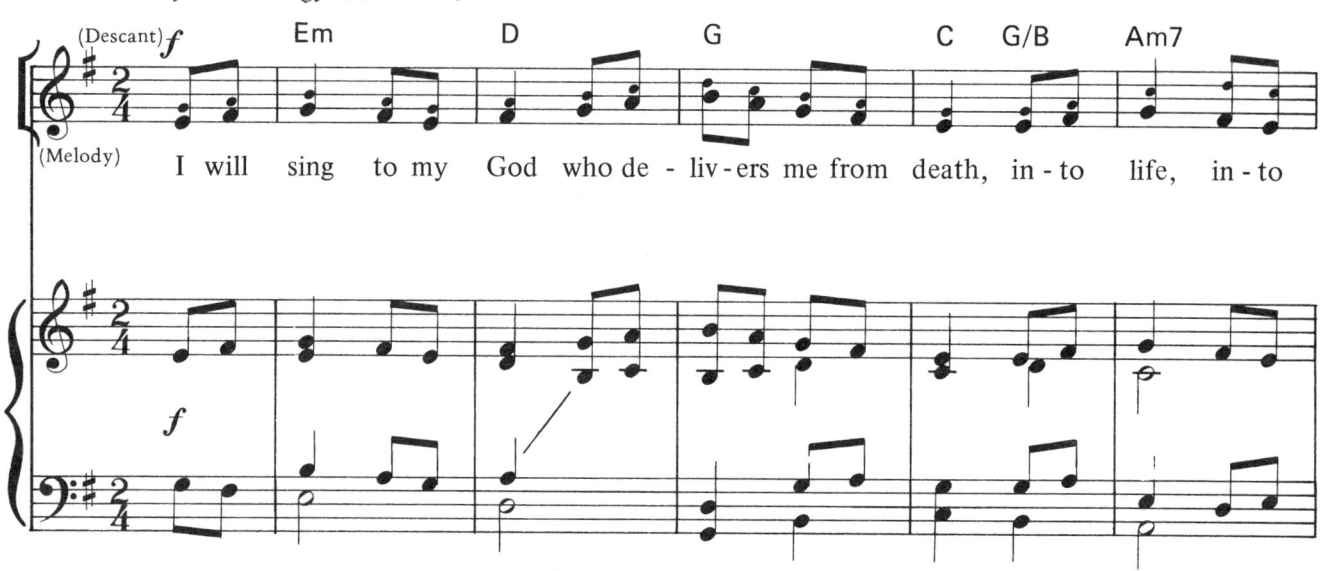

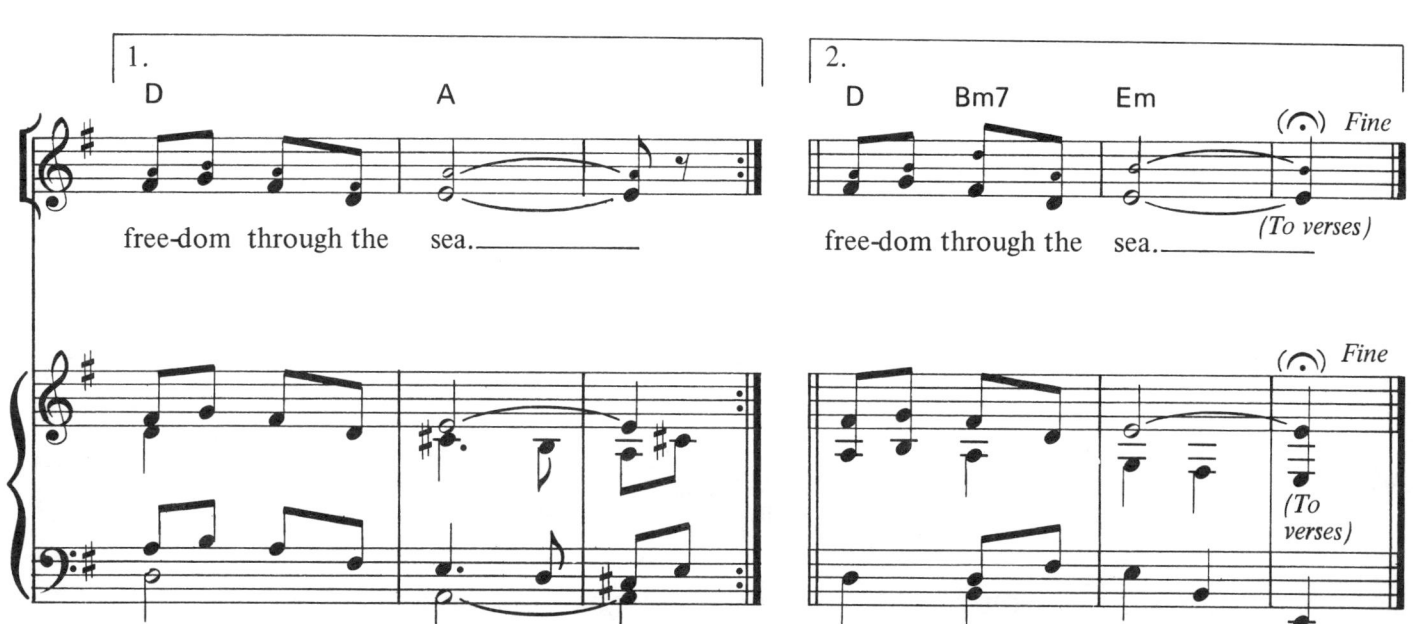

© 1988 by G.I.A. Publications, Inc. All Rights Reserved.

VERSES:

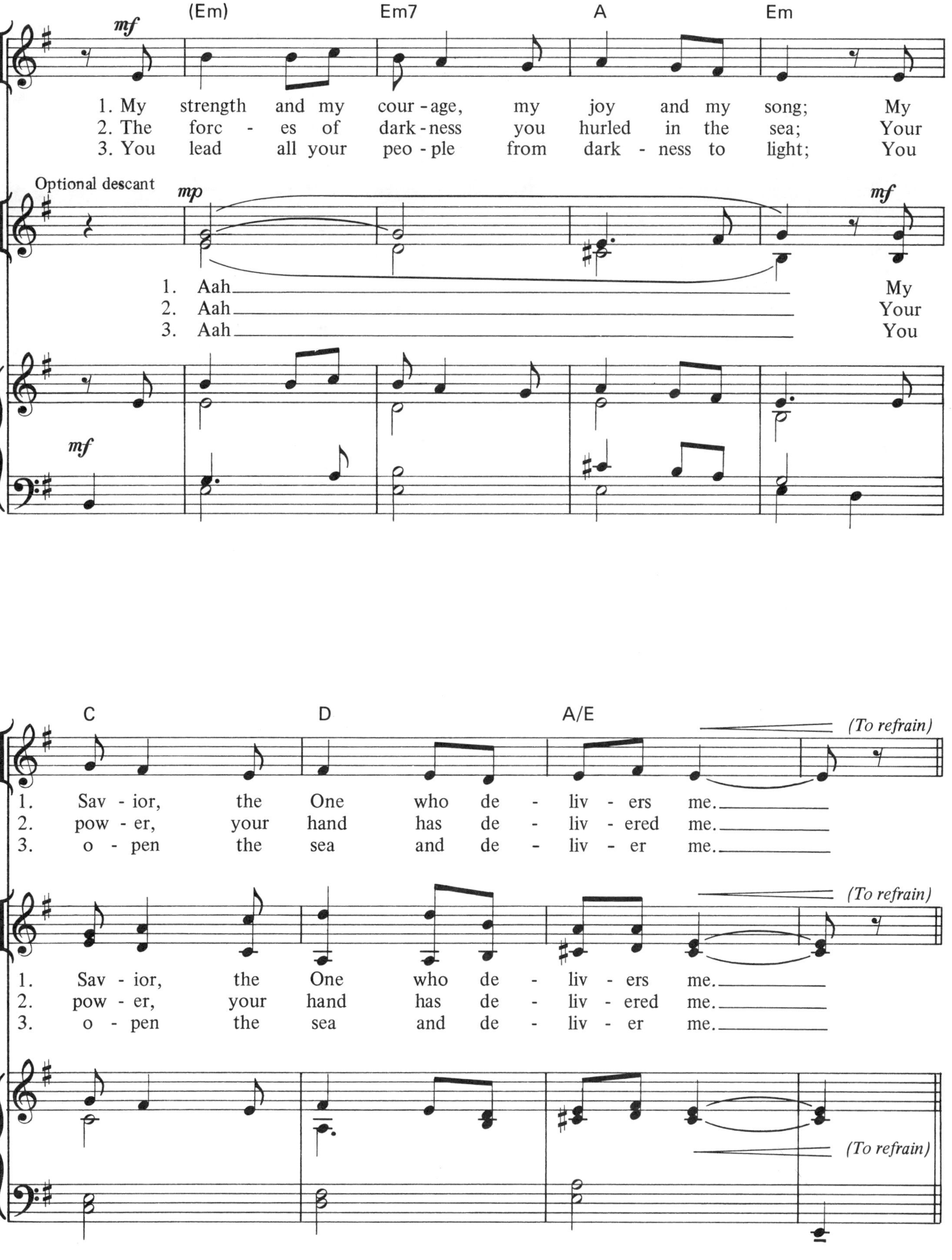
(Em) Em7 A Em
mf
1. My strength and my cour - age, my joy and my song; My
2. The forc - es of dark - ness you hurled in the sea; Your
3. You lead all your peo - ple from dark - ness to light; You
Optional descant
mp
mf
1. Aah My
2. Aah Your
3. Aah You
mf
C D A/E
(To refrain)
1. Sav - ior, the One who de - liv - ers me.
2. pow - er, your hand has de - liv - ered me.
3. o - pen the sea and de - liv - er me.
(To refrain)
1. Sav - ior, the One who de - liv - ers me.
2. pow - er, your hand has de - liv - ered me.
3. o - pen the sea and de - liv - er me.
(To refrain)

WITH JOY YOU SHALL DRAW WATER

Isaiah 12
Marty Haugen

REFRAIN: Brightly (♩ = 100-104)

© 1988 by G.I.A. Publications, Inc. All Rights Reserved.

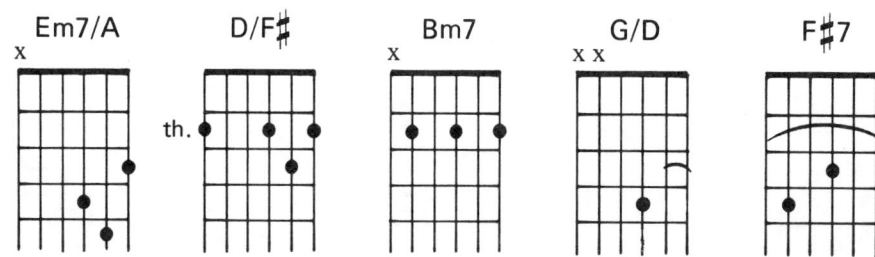

CHORDS FOR "WITH JOY YOU SHALL DRAW WATER"

MY SOUL PROCLAIMS YOUR GREATNESS

Luke 1
Marty Haugen

© 1988 by G.I.A. Publications, Inc. All Rights Reserved.

THE ORIGINAL PURCHASER OF THIS EDITION - presuming that sufficient copies have been purchased for choir, cantor, organist, instrumentalists, etc. - is authorized to photoduplicate the material printed in this box for use solely by his/her own parish/community. This authorization is only for assembly use, and only for disposable service bulletins. The entire contents (but not the box itself) must be reproduced. Removal of the title, writer's name or copyright notice is prohibited, although they may be reset to match the type style of the remainder of the bulletin material. Written permission must be obtained for all other uses.